How
Healthy
Is Your
Spirituality?

Peter Scazzero

ZONDERVAN

How Healthy Is Your Spirituality?
Copyright © 2019 by Peter Scazzero

Requests for information should be addressed to:
Zondervan, *3900 Sparks Dr. SE, Grand Rapids, Michigan 49546*

ISBN 978-0-310-35665-3 (softcover)
ISBN 978-0-310-35667-7 (audio)
ISBN 978-0-310-35666-0 (ebook)

Cover photo: Shutterstock/MaLija
Interior illustration: 123RF® / Ion Popa

First printing November 2018 / Printed in the United States of America

Contents

The Problem of Emotionally Unhealthy Spirituality

Something Is Desperately Wrong

A lack of emotional health in the early years of my ministry almost cost me everything—my marriage, my family, my work, and my own well-being. Just as my ministry leadership seemed to be reaching full swing, Geri, my wife, slowly began to protest that something was desperately wrong—wrong with me and wrong with the church. I knew she might be right so I kept trying to implement different discipleship emphases that, to a certain degree, helped me. My conversation with myself went something like this:

"More Bible study, Pete. That will change people. Their minds will be renewed. Changed lives will follow."

"No. It is body life. Get everyone in deeper levels of community, in small groups. That will do it!"

"Pete, remember, deep change requires the power of the Spirit. That can only come through prayer. Spend more time in prayer yourself and schedule more prayer meetings at New Life. God doesn't move unless we pray."

"No, these are spiritual warfare issues. The reason people aren't really changing is you are not confronting the demonic powers in and around them. Apply Scripture and pray in Jesus' authority for people to be set free from the evil one."

"Worship. That's it. If people will only soak in the presence of God in worship, that will work."

"Remember Christ's words from Matthew 25:40. We meet Christ when we give freely to 'the least of these brothers and sisters of mine,' those sick, unknown, in prison. Get them involved in serving among the poor; they will change."

"No, Pete, you need people who hear God in an exceptional way and have prophetic insight. They will finally break the unseen chains around people."

"Enough, Pete. People don't really understand the grace of God in the gospel. Our standing before God is based on Jesus' record and performance, not our own. It is his righteousness, not ours! Pound it into their heads every day, as Luther said, and they'll change!"

There is biblical truth in each of these perspectives. I believe all of them have a place in our spiritual journey and development. You, no doubt, have experienced God and his presence through one or more of these in your walk with Christ.

The problem, however, is that you inevitably find, as I

did, something is still missing. In fact, the spirituality of most current discipleship models often only adds an additional protective layer against people growing up emotionally. When people have authentic spiritual experiences—such as worship, prayer, Bible studies, and fellowship—they mistakenly believe they are doing fine, even if their relational life is fractured and their interior world is disordered. Their apparent "progress" then provides a spiritual reason for not doing the hard work of maturing.

They are deceived.

I know. I lived that way for almost seventeen years. Because of the spiritual growth in certain areas of my life and in those around me, I ignored the glaring signs of emotional immaturity that were everywhere in and around me.

In our more honest moments, most of us will admit that, much like an iceberg, we are made up of deep layers that exist well beneath our day-to-day awareness. As the following illustration shows, only about 10 percent of an iceberg is visible. This 10 percent represents the ways we conduct ourselves and the changes we make that others can see. We are nicer people, more respectful. We attend church and participate regularly. We "clean up our lives" somewhat by addressing any issues with alcohol and drugs to foul language to illicit behavior and beyond. We begin to pray and share Christ with others.

But the roots of who we are continue unchanged and unmoved.

Iceberg Model
What Lies Beneath the Surface

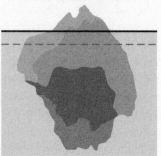

Contemporary spiritual formation and discipleship models address some of that 90 percent below the surface. The problem is that a large portion (see below the dotted line) remains untouched by Jesus Christ until there is a serious engagement with what I call "emotionally healthy spirituality."

Getting My Attention through Pain

Three things finally dragged me, kicking and screaming, to open up to the notion of emotionally healthy spirituality.

First, I was not experiencing the joy or contentment Scripture promises us in Christ. I was unhappy, frustrated, overworked, and harried. God had brought me into the Christian life with the offer, "My yoke is easy and my burden is light" (Matthew 11:30), an invitation to a free and abundant life. But I wasn't feeling it.

After many years as an active Christian, I felt exhausted and in need of a break. My life was lived more out of reaction to what other people did or might do or what they thought or might think about me. I knew in my head we were to live to please God. Living like that was another matter. Jesus' yoke felt burdensome.

Second, I was angry, bitter, and depressed. For five years I had attempted to do the work of two or three people. We had two services in English in the morning and one in the afternoon in Spanish. I preached at all of them. When my associate in our afternoon Spanish congregation left the church with two hundred of the two hundred and fifty members to start his own church, I found myself hating him. I tried, without success, to forgive him.

I experienced the growing tension of a double life— preaching love and forgiveness on Sundays and cursing alone in my car on Mondays. The gap between my beliefs and my experience now revealed itself with terrifying clarity.

Third, Geri was lonely, tired of functioning as a single mom with our four daughters. She wanted more from our marriage and grew frustrated enough to confront me. She had finally come to a place where she would not accept my excuses, delays, or avoidant behavior. She had nothing else to lose.

Late one evening, as I was sitting on our bed reading, she entered the room and calmly informed me: "Pete, I'd be happier single than married to you. I am getting off this roller coaster. I love you but refuse to live this way anymore. I have waited. . . . I have tried talking to you. You aren't listening. I can't change you. That is up to you. But I am getting on with my life."

She was resolute: "Oh, yes, by the way, the church you pastor? I quit. Your leadership isn't worth following."

For a brief moment, I understood why people murder those they love. She had exposed my nakedness. A part of me wanted to strangle her. Mostly I felt deeply ashamed. It was almost too much for my weak ego to bear.

Nonetheless, this was probably the most loving thing Geri has done for me in our entire marriage. While she could not articulate it yet at that point, she realized something vital: emotional health and spiritual maturity are inseparable. It is not possible to be spiritually mature while remaining emotionally immature. In other words, if you are touchy, unapproachable, and defensive, it doesn't matter how gifted you are, or how much Bible you know, you are, as the apostle Paul says in 1 Corinthians 13, immature.

While I sincerely loved Jesus Christ and believed many truths about him, I was an emotional infant unwilling to look at my immaturity.

Geri's leaving the church pushed me over the brink to look beneath the surface of my iceberg to depths that were, until this time, too frightening to consider. Pain has an amazing ability to open us to new truth and to get us moving. I finally acknowledged the painful truth that huge areas of my life (or iceberg, if you prefer) remained untouched by Jesus Christ. My biblical knowledge, leadership position, seminary training, experience, and skills had not changed that embarrassing reality.

I was engaged in what I now characterize as "emotionally unhealthy spirituality." I was the senior pastor of a church, but I longed to escape and join the ranks of church leavers.

Respecting Your Full Humanity

God made us as whole people, in his image (Genesis 1:27). That image includes physical, spiritual, emotional, intellectual, and social dimensions. Take a look at the following illustration:

Different Parts/Components of Who We Are

Ignoring any aspect of who we are as men and women made in God's image always results in destructive consequences—in our relationship with God, with others, and with ourselves. If you meet someone, for example, who is mentally or physically challenged, his or her lack of mental or physical development is readily apparent. An autistic child in a crowded playground standing alone for hours without interacting with other children stands out.

Emotional underdevelopment, however, is not so obvious when we first meet people. Over time, as we become involved with them, that reality becomes readily apparent.

I had ignored the "emotional component" in my seeking of God for seventeen years. The spiritual discipleship approaches of the churches and ministries that had shaped me did not have the language, theology, or training to help me in this area. It didn't matter how many books I read or seminars I attended in the other areas—physical, social, intellectual, spiritual. It didn't matter how many years passed, whether seventeen or another thirty. I would remain an emotional infant until this was exposed and transformed through Jesus Christ. The spiritual foundation upon which I had built my life (and had taught others) was cracked. There was no hiding it from those closest to me.

When I finally discovered the link between emotional maturity and spiritual maturity, a Copernican revolution began for me and there was no going back. And I don't use the word *revolution* lightly. The spiritual pathway to emotionally healthy spirituality is radical. It cuts to the root of everything about our lives, including our entire approach to following Jesus.

Making the link between emotional and spiritual maturity transformed my personal journey with Christ, my marriage, parenting, and, ultimately, New Life Fellowship Church. If you accept the invitation to embark on this path, it will do the same for you. And only a revolution in the way we follow Jesus will bring about the profound and lasting change we long for in our lives. Without that kind of change, we're likely to find ourselves trapped in a spiritual rut similar to the one Jay, one of our church members, once described to me: "I was a Christian for twenty-two years. But instead of being a twenty-two-year-old Christian, I was a one-year-old Christian twenty-two times! I just kept doing the same things over and over and over again."

Perhaps you can relate to Jay's statement, or to some of what I've shared about my own journey. Or perhaps this is all new to you. Whatever the case, I encourage you to complete the assessment beginning on page 66 before reading on. Your responses will give you a good indication about your current level of spiritual and emotional maturity, and provide a starting point for recognizing any symptoms of emotionally unhealthy spirituality in your own life.

Diagnosing the Problem: The Top Ten Symptoms of Emotionally Unhealthy Spirituality

What exactly are the indicators, or symptoms, of an emotionally unhealthy spirituality? Before we explore the pathway that leads us out of our ruts and into a healthy spirituality, it is essential to clearly identify the primary symptoms of emotionally *unhealthy* spirituality—the patterns of thought and behavior that dig the ruts in the first place and then wreak havoc in our personal lives and our churches.

In short order, here are the top ten symptoms of emotionally *unhealthy* spirituality:

1. Using God to run from God
2. Ignoring anger, sadness, and fear
3. Dying to the wrong things
4. Denying the impact of the past on the present
5. Dividing life into "secular" and "sacred" compartments
6. Doing *for* God instead of being *with* God
7. Spiritualizing away conflict
8. Covering over brokenness, weakness, and failure
9. Living without limits
10. Judging other people's spiritual journey

1. *Using God to Run from God*

Few killer viruses are more difficult to discern than this one. On the surface, all appears to be healthy and working well, but it's not. This virus hides behind hours and hours spent reading one Christian book after another . . . engaging in endless Christian responsibilities outside the home . . . all that extra time devoted to prayer and Bible study. You might wonder how such things could be anything but good for the soul. Such Christian activities become detrimental when we use them in an unconscious attempt to escape pain.

In my case, using God to run from God happens when I create a great deal of "God-activity" in order to avoid difficult areas in my life God wants to change. I know I'm in trouble when I . . .

- Do God's work to satisfy me, not him
- Do things in God's name he never asked me to do
- Pray about God doing my will, not about me surrendering to his will
- Demonstrate "Christian behaviors" so significant people think well of me
- Focus on certain theological points out of concern for my fears and unresolved emotional issues rather than out of concern for God's truth
- Use biblical truth to judge and devalue others
- Exaggerate my accomplishments for God to subtly compete with others

- Make pronouncements like, "The Lord told me I should do this," when the truth is, "I *think* the Lord told me to do this"
- Use Scripture to justify the sinful parts of my family relationships, cultural values, and national policies, instead of evaluating them under God's lordship
- Hide behind God talk, deflecting the spotlight from my inner cracks, and become defensive about my failures
- Apply biblical truths selectively to avoid anything that would require making significant life changes

How about an example? John uses God to validate his strong opinions on issues ranging from the appropriate length of women's skirts in church to political candidates to gender roles to his inability to negotiate issues with fellow non-Christian managers at work. He does not listen to or check out the innumerable assumptions he makes about others. He quickly jumps to conclusions. His friends, family, and coworkers find him unsafe and condescending.

John then goes on to convince himself he is doing God's work by misapplying selected verses of Scripture. "Of course that person hates me," he says to himself. "All those who desire to be godly will suffer persecution." Ultimately, however, he is using God to run from God.

2. Ignoring Anger, Sadness, and Fear

Many Christians believe wholeheartedly that anger, sadness, and fear are sins to be avoided. When we feel these emotions, we're sure it's an indication that something is wrong with our spiritual life. Anger is dangerous and unloving toward others. Sadness indicates a lack of faith in the promises of God; depression surely reveals a life outside the will of God! And fear? The Bible is filled with commands to "not be anxious about anything" and "do not fear" (Philippians 4:6 and Isaiah 41:10).

So what do we do? We inflate ourselves with a false confidence to make those feelings go away. We quote Scripture, pray Scripture, and memorize Scripture—anything to keep ourselves from being overwhelmed by those feelings!

Like most Christians, I was taught that almost all feelings are unreliable and not to be trusted. They go up and down and are the last thing we should be attending to in our spiritual lives. It is true that some Christians live in the extreme of following their feelings in an unhealthy, unbiblical way. It is more common, however, to encounter Christians who do not believe they have permission to admit their feelings or express them openly. This applies especially to such "difficult" feelings as fear, sadness, shame, anger, hurt, and pain. And yet, how can we listen to what God is saying and evaluate what is going on inside when we cut ourselves off from our emotions?

To feel is to be human. To minimize or deny what we feel is a distortion of what it means to be image bearers of God. To the degree that we are unable to express our emotions, we remain impaired in our ability to love God, others, and ourselves well. Why? Because our feelings are a component of what it means to be made in the image of God. To cut them out of our spirituality is to slice off an essential part of our humanity.

To support what I mistakenly believed about God and my feelings I misapplied the following illustration:[1]

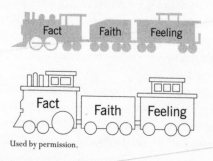

Used by permission.

I thought my spiritual life should head down the tracks beginning with the engine called "fact," which is what God said in Scripture. If I felt angry, for example, I needed to start with fact: "What are you angry about, Pete? So this person lied to you and cheated you. God is on the throne. Jesus was lied to and cheated too. So stop the anger."

After considering the fact of God's truth, I then

considered my faith—the issue of my will. Did I choose to place my faith in the fact of God's Word? Or did I follow my feelings and "fleshly" inclinations, which were not to be trusted?

At the end of the train was the caboose and what was to be trusted least—my feelings. "Under no circumstances, Pete, rely on your feelings. The heart is sinful and desperately wicked. Who can understand it [see Jeremiah 17:9]? This will only lead you astray into sin."

When taken in its entirety, the practical implications of such an imbalanced and narrow belief system are, as we shall see later, enormous—a devaluing and repression of what it means to be both human and made in the image of God. Sadly, some of our misguided Christian beliefs and expectations have, as Thomas Merton wrote, "merely deadened our humanity, instead of setting it free to develop richly, in all its capacities, under the influence of grace."[2]

3. Dying to the Wrong Things

As Iraneus said many centuries ago, "The glory of God is a human being fully alive."

True, Jesus did say, "Whoever wants to be my disciple must deny themselves and take up their cross daily and follow me" (Luke 9:23). But when we apply this verse rigidly, without qualification from the rest of Scripture, it leads to the very opposite of what God intends. It results in a narrow, faulty theology that says, "The more miserable you are, the more you suffer, the more God loves you. Disregard your unique personhood; it has no place in God's kingdom."

We are to die to the sinful parts of who we are—such as defensiveness, detachment from others, arrogance, stubbornness, hypocrisy, judgmentalism, a lack of vulnerability—as well as the more obvious sins: Do not murder. Do not steal. Do not bear false witness. Speak the truth (Exodus 20:13–16 and Ephesians 4:25).

We are not called by God to die to the "good" parts of who we are. God never asked us to die to the healthy desires and pleasures of life—to friendships, joy, art, music, beauty, recreation, laughter, and nature. God plants desires in our hearts so we will nurture and enjoy them. Often these desires and passions are invitations from God, gifts from him. Yet somehow we feel guilty unwrapping these presents.

When I ask people, "Tell me about your wishes, hopes, and dreams," they are often speechless.

"Why do you ask?" they respond. "Isn't my only wish, hope, and dream supposed to be to serve Jesus?"

Not exactly. God never asks us to annihilate the self. We are not to become "non-persons" when we become Christians. The very opposite is true. God intends our deeper, truer self, which he created, to blossom as we follow him. God has endowed each of us with certain essential qualities that reflect and express him in a unique way. In fact, an essential part of the sanctification process—becoming more like Jesus—is allowing the Holy Spirit to strip away the false constructs we have accumulated so our true selves in Christ can emerge.

4. Denying the Impact of the Past on the Present

When we come to faith in Jesus Christ, whether as a child, teenager, or adult, we are, in the dramatic language of the Bible, "born again" (John 3:3). The apostle Paul describes it this way: "The old has gone, the new is here!" (2 Corinthians 5:17).

These two verses and their meanings, however, are sometimes misunderstood. Yes, it is true that when we come to Christ, our sins are wiped away and we are given a new name, a new identity, a new future, a new life. It is truly a miracle. We are declared righteous before God through the life, death, and resurrection of Jesus (Philippians 3:9–10). The eternal, holy God of the universe is no longer our judge but our Father. That is the great news of the gospel. But we need to understand this does not mean that our past won't continue to influence us in different ways. For years, I was under the delusion that because I accepted Jesus, my old life was no longer in me. My past before Christ was painful. I wanted to forget it. I never wanted to look back. Life was so much better now that Jesus was with me.

I thought I was free.

Geri, after nine years of marriage, knew better. I will never forget the first time we made a genogram—a diagram outlining some of the patterns of our families. Our counselor at the time took about an hour to ask probing questions about the interactions between members of both of our families, to write two or three adjectives to describe our parents and their relationships.

When the counselor finished, he simply asked us, "Do you see any similarities between your marriage and your parents'?"

We both sat there dumbfounded.

We were evangelical Christians. We were committed and stable. Our priorities and life choices were very different from that of our parents'. Yet, underneath the surface, our marriage bore a striking resemblance to that of our parents'. Gender roles; the handling of anger and conflict and shame; how we defined success; our view of family, children, recreation, pleasure, sexuality, grieving; and our relationships with friends had all been shaped by our families of origin and our cultures.

Sitting in that counselor's office that day, embarrassed by the state of our marriage, we learned a lesson we would never forget: even though we had been committed Christians for almost twenty years, our ways of relating mirrored much more our family of origin than the way God intended for his new family in Christ.

The work of growing in Christ (what theologians

call *sanctification*) does not mean we don't go back to the past as we press ahead to what God has for us. It actually demands we go back in order to break free from unhealthy and destructive patterns that prevent us from loving ourselves and others as God designed.

5. Dividing Life into "Secular" and "Sacred" Compartments

Human beings have an uncanny ability to live compartmentalized, double lives.

Frank attends church and sings about God's love. On the way home he pronounces the death penalty over another driver. For Frank, Sunday church is for God. Monday to Saturday is for work.

Jane yells at her husband, berating him for his lack of spiritual leadership with the children. He walks away deflated and crushed. She walks away convinced she has fought valiantly in God's name.

Ken has a disciplined devotional time with God each day before going to work, but then does not think of God's presence with him all through the day at work or when he returns home to be with his wife and children.

Judith cries during songs about the love and grace of God at her church. But she regularly complains and blames others for the difficulties and trials in her life.

It is so easy to compartmentalize God, relegating him to "Christian activities" around church and our spiritual disciplines without thinking of him in the way we navigate our marriages, discipline our children, spend our money, enjoy our recreation, or even study for exams. According to Gallup polls and sociologists, one of the greatest scandals of our day is that "evangelical Christians are as likely to embrace lifestyles every bit as hedonistic, materialistic, self-centered and sexually immoral as the world in general."[3] The statistics are devastating:

- Church members divorce their spouses as often as their secular neighbors.
- Church members beat their wives as often as their neighbors.
- Church members' giving patterns indicate they are almost as materialistic as non-Christians.
- White evangelicals are the most likely people to object to neighbors of another race.
- Of the "higher-commitment" evangelicals, a rapidly growing number of young people think cohabitation is acceptable prior to marriage.[4]

Ron Sider, in his book *The Scandal of the Evangelical Conscience*, summarizes the level of our compartmentalization: "Whether the issue is marriage and sexuality or money and care for the poor, evangelicals today are living scandalously unbiblical lives. . . . The data suggest that in many crucial areas evangelicals are not living any differently from their unbelieving neighbors."[5] But you don't need a lot of statistics to know how true this is. Just ask Angela, a new member of our congregation whose question to me also explained why she had dropped out of church for five years: "Why is it that so many Christians make such lousy human beings?"

The consequences of this on our witness to Jesus Christ are incalculable, both for ourselves and the world around us. We miss out on the genuine joy of life with Jesus Christ that he promises (John 15:11). And the watching world shakes its head, incredulous that we can be so blind we can't see the large gap between our words and our everyday lives.

6. *Doing* for *God Instead of Being* with *God*

Being productive and getting things done are high priorities in Western culture. Praying and enjoying God's presence for no other reason than to delight in him was a luxury, I was told, that we could take pleasure in once we got to heaven. For now, there was too much to be done. People were lost. The world was in deep trouble. And God had entrusted us with the good news of the gospel.

For most of my Christian life, I wondered if monks were truly Christian. Their lifestyle seemed escapist. Surely they were not in the will of God. What were they doing to spread the gospel in a world dying without Christ? What about all the sheep who were lost and without direction? Didn't they know the laborers are few (Matthew 9:37)?

The messages were clear:

- Doing lots of work for God is a sure sign of a growing spirituality.
- It is all up to you. And you'll never finish while you're alive on earth.
- God can't move unless you pray.
- You are responsible to share Christ around you at all times or people will go to hell.
- Things will fall apart if you don't persevere and hold things together.

Are all these things wrong? No. But work *for* God that is not nourished by a deep interior life *with* God will eventually be contaminated by other things such as ego, power, needing approval of and from others, and buying into the wrong ideas of success and the mistaken belief that we can't fail. When we work for God because of these things, our experience of the gospel often falls off center. We become "human doings," not "human beings." Our experiential sense of worth and validation gradually shifts from God's unconditional love for us in Christ to our works and performance. The joy of Christ gradually disappears. Our activity for God can only properly flow from a life *with* God.

We cannot give what we do not possess. Doing for God in a way that is proportionate to our being with God is the only pathway to a pure heart and seeing God (Matthew 5:8).

7. Spiritualizing Away Conflict

Nobody likes conflict. Yet conflict is everywhere—from law courts to workplaces to classrooms to neighborhoods to marriages to parenting our children to close friendships to when someone has spoken or acted toward you inappropriately. But perhaps one of the most destructive myths alive in the Christian community today is the belief that smoothing over disagreements or "sweeping them under the rug" is part of what it means to follow Jesus. For this reason, churches, small groups, ministry teams, denominations, and communities continue to experience the pain of unresolved conflicts.

Very, very few of us come from families in which conflicts are resolved in a mature, healthy way. Most of us simply bury our tensions and move on. When I became a Christian I also became the great "peacemaker." I did anything to keep unity and love flowing in the church as well as in my marriage and family. I saw conflict as something that had to be fixed as quickly as possible. Like radioactive waste from a nuclear power plant, if not contained, I feared it might unleash terrible damage.

So I did what most Christians do: I lied a lot, both to myself and others.

What do you do when faced with the tension and mess of disagreements? Some of us may be guilty of one or more of the following:

- Say one thing to people's faces and then another behind their backs
- Make promises we have no intention of keeping
- Blame
- Attack
- Give people the silent treatment
- Become sarcastic
- Give in because we are afraid of not being liked
- "Leak" our anger by sending an email containing a not-so-subtle criticism
- Tell only half the truth because we can't bear to hurt a friend's feelings
- Say yes when we mean no
- Avoid and withdraw and cut off
- Find an outside person with whom we can share in order to ease our anxiety

Jesus shows us that healthy Christians do not avoid conflict. His life was filled with it! He was in regular conflict with the religious leaders, the crowds, the disciples—even his own family. Out of a desire to bring true peace, Jesus disrupted the false peace all around him. He refused to spiritualize conflict avoidance.

8. Covering Over Brokenness, Weakness, and Failure

The pressure to present an image of ourselves as strong and spiritually "together" hovers over most of us. We feel guilty for not measuring up, for not making the grade. We forget that not one of us is perfect and that we are all sinners. We forget that David, one of God's most beloved friends, committed adultery with Bathsheba and murdered her husband. Talk about a scandal! How many of us would not have erased that from the history books forever lest the name of God be disgraced?

David did not. Instead, he used his absolute power as king to ensure the details of his colossal failure were published in the history books for all future generations! In fact, David wrote a song about his failure to be sung in Israel's worship services and to be published in their worship manual, the psalms. (Hopefully, he asked Bathsheba's permission first!) David knew, "My sacrifice, O God, is a broken spirit; a broken and contrite heart you, God, will not despise" (Psalm 51:17).

Another of God's great men, the apostle Paul, wrote about God not answering his prayers and about his "thorn in [the] flesh." He thanked God for his brokenness, reminding his readers that Christ's power "is made perfect in weakness" (2 Corinthians 12:7–10).

How many Christians do you know who would do such a thing today?

The Bible does not spin the flaws and weaknesses of its heroes. Moses was a murderer. Hosea's wife was a prostitute. Peter rebuked God! Noah got drunk. Jonah was a racist. Jacob was a liar. John Mark deserted Paul. Elijah burned out. Jeremiah was depressed and suicidal. Thomas doubted. Moses had a temper. Timothy had ulcers. And all these people send the same message: that every human being on earth, regardless of their gifts and strengths, is weak, vulnerable, and dependent on God and others.

For years I would observe unusually gifted people perform in extraordinary ways—whether in the arts, sports, leadership, politics, business, academics, parenting, or church—and wonder if somehow they had escaped the brokenness that plagues the rest of us. Now I know they hadn't. We are all deeply flawed and broken. There are no exceptions.

9. Living Without Limits

I was taught that good Christians constantly give and tend to the needs of others. I wasn't supposed to say no to opportunities to help or to requests for help because that would be selfish.

Some Christians are selfish. They believe in God and Jesus Christ but live their lives as if God doesn't exist.

They don't think or care about loving and serving others outside of their families and friends. That is a tragedy.

I meet many more Christians, however, who carry around guilt for never doing enough. "Pete, I spent two hours on the phone listening to him and it still wasn't enough," a friend recently complained to me. "It makes me want to run away."

This guilt often leads to discouragement. And this discouragement often leads Christians to disengagement and isolation from "needy people" because they don't know what else to do.

The core spiritual issue here relates to our limits and our humanity. We are not God. We cannot serve everyone in need. We are human. When Paul said, "I can do all this through him who gives me strength" (Philippians 4:13), the context was that of learning to be content in all circumstances. The strength he received from Christ was not the strength to change, deny, or defy his circumstances; it was the strength to be content in the midst of them, to surrender to God's loving will for him (Philippians 4:11–13).

Jesus modeled this for us as a human being—fully God yet fully human. He did not heal every sick person in Palestine. He did not raise every dead person. He did not feed all the hungry beggars or set up job development centers for the poor of Jerusalem.

He didn't do it, and we shouldn't feel we have to.

But somehow we do. Why don't we take appropriate care of ourselves? Why are so many Christians, along with the rest of our culture, frantic, exhausted, overloaded, and hurried?

Few Christians make the connection between love of self and love of others. Sadly, many believe that taking care of themselves is a sin, a "psychologizing" of the gospel taken from our self-centered culture. I believed that myself for years.

It is true we are called to consider others more important than ourselves (Philippians 2:3). We are called to lay down our lives for others (1 John 3:16). But remember, you first need a "self" to lay down.

As Parker Palmer said, "Self-care is never a selfish act—it is simply good stewardship of the only gift I have, the gift I was put on earth to offer others. Anytime we can listen to true self and give it the care it requires, we do it not only for ourselves, but for the many others whose lives we touch."[6]

10. Judging Other People's Spiritual Journey

"The monk," said one of the Desert Fathers, "must die to his neighbor and never judge him at all in any way whatever." He continued: "If you are occupied with your own faults, you have no time to see those of your neighbor."[7]

I was taught it was my responsibility to correct

people in error or in sin and to always counsel people who were mixed up spiritually. I therefore felt guilty if I saw something questionable and did nothing to point it out. But I felt even guiltier when I was supposed to fix someone's problem and had to admit "I don't know how" or "I don't know what to say." Wasn't I commanded to be ready to give an answer for the hope that is in me (1 Peter 3:15)?

Of course, many of us have no trouble at all dispensing advice or pointing out wrongdoing. We spend so much time at it that we end up self-deceived, thinking we have much to give and therefore little to receive from others. After all, we're the ones who are right, aren't we? This often leads to an inability to receive from ordinary, less mature people than ourselves. We only receive from experts or professionals.

This has always been one of the greatest dangers in Christianity. It becomes "us versus them." In Jesus' day there was the superior "in group" of Pharisees who obeyed God's commands. And there was the inferior "out group" of sinners, tax collectors, and prostitutes.

Sadly, we often turn our differences into moral superiority or virtues. I see it all the time. We judge people for their music (too soft or too loud). We judge them for dressing up or dressing down, for the movies they watch and the cars they buy. We create never-ending groups to subtly categorize people:

- "Those artists and musicians. They are so flaky."
- "Those engineers. They are so cerebral. They're cold as fish."
- "Men are idiots. They're socially infantile."
- "Women are overly sensitive and emotional."
- "The rich are self-indulgent and selfish."
- "The poor are lazy."

We judge the Presbyterians for being too structured. We judge the Pentecostals for lacking structure. We judge Episcopalians for their candles and their written prayers. We judge Roman Catholics for their view of the Lord's Supper and Orthodox Christians from the Eastern part of the world for their strange culture and love for icons.

By failing to let others be themselves before God and move at their own pace, we inevitably project onto them our own discomfort with their choice to live life differently than we do. We end up eliminating them in our minds, trying to make others like us, abandoning them altogether or falling into a "Who cares?" indifference toward them. In some ways, the silence of unconcern can be more deadly than hate. Like Jesus said, unless I first take the log out of my own eye, knowing that I have huge blind spots, I am dangerous. I must see the extensive damage sin has done to every part of who I am—emotion, intellect, body, will, and spirit—before I can attempt to remove the speck from the eye of another (Matthew 7:1–5).

The Revolutionary Antidote

The pathway to unleashing the transformative power of Jesus to heal our spiritual lives is found in the joining of emotional health and contemplative, or slowed down, spirituality. Both are powerful, life-changing emphases when engaged in separately. But *together* they offer nothing short of a spiritual revolution, transforming the hidden places deep beneath the surface. When emotional health and contemplative spirituality are interwoven together in an individual's life, a small group, a church, a university fellowship, or a community, people's lives are dramatically transformed. They work as an antidote to heal the ten symptoms of emotionally unhealthy spirituality.

Defining Emotional Health and Contemplative Spirituality

So what exactly are emotional health and contemplative spirituality? Let's take a closer look at each one.

Emotional health is concerned with such things as:[8]

- naming, recognizing, and managing our own feelings;
- identifying with and having active compassion for others;
- initiating and maintaining close and meaningful relationships;

- breaking free from self-destructive patterns;
- being aware of how our past impacts our present;
- developing the capacity to express our thoughts and feelings clearly;
- respecting and loving others without having to change them;
- asking for what we need, want, or prefer clearly, directly, and respectfully;
- accurately self-assessing our strengths, limits, and weaknesses and freely sharing them with others;
- learning the capacity to resolve conflict maturely and negotiate solutions that consider the perspectives of others;
- integrating our spirituality with our sexuality in a healthy way;
- grieving well.

Contemplative spirituality, on the other hand, is concerned with slowing down to be with God, focusing on such practices as:[9]

- awakening and surrendering to God's love in any and every situation;
- positioning ourselves to hear God and remember his presence in all we do;
- communing with God, allowing him to fully indwell the depth of our being;

- practicing silence, solitude, and a life of unceasing prayer;
- resting attentively in the presence of God;
- understanding our earthly life as a journey of transformation toward ever-increasing union with God;
- finding the true essence of who we are in God;
- loving others out of a life of love for God;
- developing a balanced, harmonious rhythm of life that enables us to be aware of the sacred in all of life;
- adapting historic practices of spirituality that are applicable today;
- allowing our Christian lives to be shaped by the rhythms of the Christian calendar rather than the culture; and
- living in committed community that passionately loves Jesus above all else.

The combination of emotional health and contemplative spirituality addresses what I believe to be the missing piece in much of contemporary Christianity. When practiced together, they unleash the Holy Spirit inside us in order that we might know experientially the power of an authentic life in Christ.

Emotional health and contemplation are different and yet overlap. Both are necessary for loving God, loving

ourselves, and loving others. The greatest command-
ments, Jesus said, are that we love God with all our heart,
mind, strength, and soul and that we love our neighbor as
ourselves (Matthew 22:37–40). Contemplation, or what
I call slowed-down spirituality, has been defined in many
ways throughout history. Brother Lawrence called it "the
pure loving gaze that finds God everywhere." Francis
de Sales described it as "the mind's loving, unmixed,
permanent attention to the things of God." We are not
simply about experiencing a better quality of life through
emotional health. Awareness of and responding to the
love of God is at the heart of our lives. We are first and
foremost about God revealed in Christ.

At the same time, contemplation is not simply about
our relationship with God. It is ultimately the way we see
and treat people and the way we look at ourselves. Our
relationship with God and relationship with others are
two sides of the same coin. If our contemplation or "loving
union with God" does not result in a loving union with
people, then it is, as 1 John 4:7–21 says so eloquently, not
true. Moreover, it is about seeing God in *all* of life, not
just in what we might consider the spiritual aspects of life.

Emotional health, on the other hand, concerns itself
primarily with loving others well. It connects us to our
interior life, making possible the seeing and treating
of each individual as worthy of respect, created in the
image of God and not just as an object to use. For this

reason, self-awareness—knowing what is going on inside of us—is indispensable to emotional health and loving well. In fact, the extent to which we love and respect ourselves is the extent to which we will be able to love and respect others.

At the same time, emotional health is not only about ourselves and our relationships. It also impacts our image of God, including our ability to hear God's voice and discern his will.

Allow me to share a personal story that illustrates how the tools of *both* emotional health and contemplative spirituality are essential to truly break free from our dysfunctions and illusions. I worked for several years on understanding the impact my family history had on my present relationships. While in an advanced program in marriage and family, my class was given the assignment of interviewing every living member of our families. The goal was to put together the jigsaw puzzle of our family history, to uncover any secrets, and to understand ourselves more accurately within the context of our families. God used that experience to make me aware of numerous generational patterns that negatively impacted my relationship with Geri, our daughters, my coworkers at New Life Fellowship, and myself. By the power of the Holy Spirit, I was able to make specific positive changes for Christ.

Two years later, during a lengthy time of silence and

solitude (one of the gifts of contemplative spirituality), I found myself feeling angry at God. I not only yelled at God, I cursed him! I called him a liar. "Your yoke is not easy and light!" I screamed aloud. (Don't worry. I was by myself.) And even though I felt angry, I wondered where the anger was coming from.

This led me to weeks of meditating and pondering Jesus' invitation: "Come to me, all you who are weary and burdened, and I will give you rest. . . . For my yoke is easy and my burden is light" (Matthew 11:28, 30). Over time, I realized that underneath my preaching countless sermons on God's grace and love, I perceived God as a perfectionist—a demanding taskmaster. But was it really him? Or was it part of my past I was unwilling to look at?

I came to realize during this time of solitude that the god I was serving reflected my earthly parents more than the God of Scripture. "I am never enough," was how I often felt in my family growing up. Almost unconsciously, I had transferred that perspective to my heavenly Father. No matter what I did, all I could hear God saying to me was, "It is never enough, Pete." I had never made that connection before.

I was stunned!

My point is this: There are powerful breakthroughs that can take place deep below the surface of our lives when the riches of both contemplative spirituality *and* emotional health are joined together. I have seen this again and again in my own life and in the lives of countless others. Together, they form a refining fire in which God's love burns away what is false and unreal and his fierce and purifying love sets us free to live in the truth of Jesus.

IF YOU WANT TO LEARN MORE

This booklet was drawn from a book I wrote called *Emotionally Healthy Spirituality: It's Impossible to Be Spiritually Mature, While Remaining Emotionally Immature*. If what you've read here has awakened in you hunger for deeper healing and growth, I encourage you to continue your journey by reading *Emotionally Healthy Spirituality*. To help individuals and churches experience this level of transformation, we developed a course based on this book called The Emotionally Healthy (EH) Discipleship Course. For more information on this and other EHS resources, visit www.emotionalyhealthy.org.

To help you take your next steps, the following pages include an excerpt from an EHS devotional book called *Emotionally Healthy Spirituality Day by Day*.

Wherever your next steps take you, my prayer is that God will give you the courage to faithfully live your unique life in Christ, and that you will discover a whole new way of living as a result. May his love invade you as you continue your journey. The love of God will never fail to teach you what you must do.

Excerpt from
Emotionally Healthy
Spirituality Day by Day

*E*motionally Healthy Spirituality Day by Day introduces a revolutionary spiritual discipline called the "Daily Office," which provides a structured way to be with God and spend time with him each day.

The goal of the Daily Office is to pay attention to God throughout the entire day *while we are active*, which is one way it differs from what we refer to today as "quiet time" or "devotions." Quiet time and devotions normally take place once a day, usually in the morning, and focus on "getting filled up" for the day or interceding for the needs of others. The Daily Office takes place at least twice a day, and it is not so much about turning to God to *get* something as it is turning to God to simply be *with* him.

The sample Offices included here are taken from Week One, "The Problem of Emotionally Unhealthy

Spirituality." Each Office includes the following five elements:

1. Silence, Stillness, and Centering
2. Scripture
3. Devotional Reading
4. Question to Consider
5. Prayer

You choose the length of time for your Offices. The key, remember, is the regular remembrance of God, not the length of time. Your pausing to be with God might last anywhere from two minutes to twenty minutes to forty-five minutes.

As you begin your journey with the Daily Office, I encourage you to allow a lot of time and practice to make progress in this. Few of us have life-giving rhythms, so rearranging our days to stop and be with Jesus is a major shift. Add to this the reality that little silence exists in the culture, our families of origin, even in our churches and the challenge can feel overwhelming. But I can assure you that if you will persevere and ask the Holy Spirit for help, you will find that God has been waiting for you. You will get to know him in ways that can happen only in silence (Psalm 46:10). Your listening-to-God "muscles" may develop slowly, but they will develop. By God's grace, your capacity to be with Jesus will enlarge and expand. Your relationships will change, with more of Jesus flowing out of you and less of the bad patterns you may have learned from the culture or your family of origin. But most importantly, you will discover, as millions of others have across the ages, that his love really is better than life (Psalm 63:3).

The Problem of
Emotionally Unhealthy
Spirituality

DAILY OFFICES
Week One

Day 1: Morning/Midday Office

Silence and Stillness before God (2 minutes)

Scripture Reading: Mark 11:15–17

> On reaching Jerusalem, Jesus entered the temple
> courts and began driving out those who were buying
> and selling there. He overturned the tables of the
> money changers and the benches of those selling doves,
> and would not allow anyone to carry merchandise
> through the temple courts. And as he taught them,
> he said, "Is it not written: 'My house will be called a
> house of prayer for all nations'? But you have made it
> 'a den of robbers.'"

Devotional

Jesus' intense anger and overturning of the tables in the
temple courts ought to make us gasp. He knows that if
we don't get to God, invaluable treasures will be lost
or obscured. We lose the space where we experience
God's unfailing love and amazing forgiveness. We lose
an eternal perspective on what is important and what
is not. We lose compassion. We gain the world but lose
our souls (Mark 8:36–37).

Be Free for God

I have a need
of such clearance
as the Savior effected in the temple of Jerusalem
a riddance of clutter
of what is secondary
that blocks the way
to the all-important central emptiness
which is filled
with the presence of God alone.

—*Jean Danielou*[1]

Question to Consider

How would you describe "what is secondary" in your life, the thing that might be "blocking the way" to experiencing God?

Prayer

Lord, help me to see how much I lose when I lose you. My perspective on my life and all of life gets distorted when I don't make space for you, obscuring your love for me. Your love is better than life, and truly I long for more tastes of that love. In Jesus' name, amen.

Conclude with Silence (2 minutes)

Day 1: Midday/Evening Office

Silence and Stillness before God (2 minutes)

Scripture Reading: 1 Samuel 15:22–23

But Samuel replied:

"Does the LORD delight in burnt offerings and sacrifices
   as much as in obeying the LORD?
To obey is better than sacrifice,
   and to heed is better than the fat of rams.
For rebellion is like the sin of divination,
   and arrogance like the evil of idolatry.
Because you have rejected the word of the LORD,
   he has rejected you as king."

Devotional

Saul, the first king of Israel, did not know much about silence or listening to God. Like David, he was a gifted, anointed, successful military/political leader. Yet unlike David, we never see him seeking to be with God. In this passage, Samuel the prophet reprimands Saul for doing many religious acts (i.e., offering burnt offerings and sacrifices) but not quieting himself enough to listen, or "to heed" God (v. 22).

We all must take the time to be silent and to contemplate, especially those who live in big cities like

London and New York, where everything moves so fast. . . . I always begin my prayer in silence, for it is in the silence of the heart that God speaks. God is the friend of silence—we need to listen to God because it's not what we say but what He says to us and through us that matters. Prayer feeds the soul—as blood is to the body, prayer is to the soul—and it brings you closer to God. It also gives you a clean and pure heart. A clean heart can see God, can speak to God, and can see the love of God in others.

—*Mother Teresa[2]*

Question to Consider

How could you make more room in your life for silence in order to listen to God?

Prayer

Unclutter my heart, O God, until I am quiet enough to hear you speak out of the silence. Help me in these few moments to stop, to listen, to wait, to be still, and to allow your presence to envelop me. In Jesus' name, amen.

Conclude with Silence (2 minutes)

Day 2: Morning/Midday Office

Silence and Stillness before God (2 minutes)

Scripture Reading: Jonah 1:1–4

The word of the LORD came to Jonah son of Amittai:
"Go to the great city of Nineveh and preach against it,
because its wickedness has come up before me."

But Jonah ran away from the LORD and headed for
Tarshish. He went down to Joppa, where he found a
ship bound for that port. After paying the fare, he went
aboard and sailed for Tarshish to flee from the LORD.

Then the LORD sent a great wind on the sea, and
such a violent storm arose that the ship threatened to
break up.

Devotional

Jonah is an example of a prophet with a case of emotionally unhealthy spirituality. He hears and serves God but
refuses to listen to God's call to love and show mercy to
Nineveh, a world power of that day known for its violent,
barbaric behavior. Jonah flees 2,400 miles in the opposite
direction, to Tarshish, in present-day Spain.

And why Tarshish? For one thing, it is a lot more exciting
than Nineveh. Nineveh was an ancient site with layer
after layer of ruined and unhappy history. Going to

Nineveh to preach was not a coveted assignment for a
Hebrew prophet with good references. But Tarshish was
something else. Tarshish was exotic. Tarshish was adven-
ture . . . Tarshish in the biblical references was a "far off
and sometimes idealized port." It is reported in 1 Kings
10:22 that Solomon's fleet of Tarshish fetched gold, sil-
ver, ivory, monkeys and peacocks. . . . In Tarshish we can
have a religious career without having to deal with God.

—*Eugene Peterson[3]*

As Jonah runs, however, God sends a great storm.
Jonah loses control of his life and destiny. He is thrown
overboard and swallowed by a great fish. It is from the belly
of the fish that Jonah begins to wrestle with God in prayer.

Question to Consider

What internal or external storm might God be sending into
your life as a sign that something is not right spiritually?

Prayer

*Lord, may your will, not my will, be done in my life. You
know how easy it is to call myself a Christian but then become
busy, forgetting about your will and desires. Forgive me for this
sin. Help me listen to you, and grant me the courage to faithfully
surrender to you. In Jesus' name, amen.*

Conclude with Silence (2 minutes)

Day 2: Midday/Evening Office

Silence and Stillness before God (2 minutes)

Scripture Reading: 1 John 2:15–17

Do not love the world or anything in the world. If anyone loves the world, love for the Father is not in them. For everything in the world—the lust of the flesh, the lust of the eyes, and the pride of life—comes not from the Father but from the world. The world and its desires pass away, but whoever does the will of God lives forever.

Devotional

At the end of the third century in the deserts of Egypt, an extraordinary phenomenon occurred. Christian men and women began to flee the cities and villages to see God in the desert. They discerned how easy it was to lose one's soul in the entanglements and manipulations found in society, so they pursued God in a radical way by moving to the desert. They became known as the "Desert Fathers."

Society . . . was regarded by them as a shipwreck from which each single individual man had to swim for his life. . . . These were men who believed that to let oneself drift along, passively accepting the tenets and values of what they knew as society, was purely and simply a disaster. . . . They knew they were helpless to do any good for others as long as they floundered about in the wreckage. But once they got a foothold on solid ground, things were different. Then they had not only the power but even the obligation to pull the whole world to safety after them.

—*Thomas Merton*[4]

Question to Consider

How do you hear the words of the apostle John today: "Do not love the world or anything in the world" (1 John 2:15)?

Prayer

Lord, in order to be with you, I need you to show me how to "create a desert" in the midst of my full, active life. Cleanse me from the pressures, illusions, and pretenses that confront me today so that my life may serve as a gift to those around me.

Conclude with Silence (2 minutes)

Day 3: Morning/Midday Office

Silence and Stillness before God (2 minutes)

Scripture Reading: Genesis 32:22–26, 30

That night Jacob got up and took his two wives, his two female servants and his eleven sons and crossed the ford of the Jabbok. After he had sent them across the stream, he sent over all his possessions. So Jacob was left alone, and a man wrestled with him till daybreak. When the man saw that he could not overpower him, he touched the socket of Jacob's hip so that his hip was wrenched as he wrestled with the man. Then the man said, "Let me go, for it is daybreak." But Jacob replied, "I will not let you go unless you bless me."

So Jacob called the place Peniel, saying, "It is because I saw God face to face, and yet my life was spared."

Devotional

Jacob's name can mean "cheat" or "grabber," and he lived up to his name. He was manipulative, deceptive, and aggressive—not someone you'd likely nominate for a leadership position in your church. Jacob was a seriously flawed person growing up in a dysfunctional family. He seemed to be either getting into trouble, just getting out of it, or about to make some more.[5]

Jacob's story is so universal because it is so personal.

Throughout his life, Jacob was stubborn and unwilling to trust anyone—even God. It was at the Jabbok brook that Jacob was finally broken by God and radically transformed. He was given a new name and a new freedom to live as God originally intended. This came, however, at the price of a permanent limp that rendered him helpless and desperate to cling to God. And it is out of this weak place of dependence that Jacob became a nation (Israel) that would bless the world.

In the same way, God sometimes wounds us in our journey with him in order to move us out of an unhealthy, "tip of the iceberg" spirituality to one that truly transforms us from the inside out. When these wounds come, we can deny them, cover them, get angry with God, blame others, or like Jacob we can cling desperately to God.

Question to Consider

In what way(s) has God put your life or plans "out of joint" so that you might depend on him?

Prayer

Father, I relate to Jacob in striving, manipulating, scheming, denying, and spinning half-truths to those around me in order to get my way. At times, I too find myself serving you in order to get something from you. Lord, I invite you to teach me to live in dependence on you. Help me to rest and be still in your love alone. In Jesus' name, amen.

Conclude with Silence (2 minutes)

Day 3: Midday/Evening Office

Silence and Stillness before God (2 minutes)

Scripture Reading: Matthew 16:21–23

From that time on Jesus began to explain to his disciples that he must go to Jerusalem and suffer many things at the hands of the elders, the chief priests and the teachers of the law, and that he must be killed and on the third day be raised to life.

Peter took him aside and began to rebuke him. "Never, Lord!" he said. "This shall never happen to you!"

Jesus turned and said to Peter, "Get behind me, Satan! You are a stumbling block to me; you do not have in mind the concerns of God, but merely human concerns."

Devotional

The apostle Peter had a passionate heart for Jesus, but he was also rash, proud, immature, and inconsistent. His impulsiveness and stubbornness are evident throughout the gospels.

Yet Jesus patiently led Peter to a crucifixion of his self-will, in order that he might experience genuine resurrection life and power.

When I am still, compulsion (the busyness that Hilary of Tours called "a blasphemous anxiety to do God's work for him") gives way to compunction (being pricked or punctured). That is, God can break through the many layers with which I protect myself, so that I can hear his Word and be poised to listen. . . .

In perpetual motion I can mistake the flow of my adrenaline for the moving of the Holy Spirit; I can live in the illusion that I am ultimately in control of my destiny and my daily affairs. . . .

French philosopher and mathematician Blaise Pascal observed that most of our human problems come because we don't know how to sit still in our room for an hour.

—*Leighton Ford*[6]

Question to Consider

What might be one way your busyness blocks you from listening and communing intimately with the living God?

Prayer

Lord, forgive me for running my life without you today. I offer my anxieties to you now—as best I can. Help me to be still, to surrender to your will, and to rest in your loving arms. In the name of the Father, the Son, and the Holy Spirit, amen.

Conclude with Silence (2 minutes)

Day 4: Morning/Midday Office

Silence and Stillness before God (2 minutes)

Scripture Reading: Luke 10:38–42

As Jesus and his disciples were on their way, he came to a village where a woman named Martha opened her home to him. She had a sister called Mary, who sat at the Lord's feet listening to what he said. But Martha was distracted by all the preparations that had to be made. She came to him and asked, "Lord, don't you care that my sister has left me to do the work by myself? Tell her to help me!"

"Martha, Martha," the Lord answered, "you are worried and upset about many things, but few things are needed—or indeed only one. Mary has chosen what is better, and it will not be taken away from her."

Devotional

Mary and Martha represent two approaches to the Christian life.

Martha is actively serving Jesus, but she is also missing Jesus. She is busy in the "doing" of life. Her life is pressured and filled with distractions. Her duties have become disconnected from her love for Jesus. Martha's problems, however, go beyond her busyness. I suspect that if Martha were to sit at the feet of Jesus, she would still be distracted by everything on her mind. Her inner person is touchy, irritable, and anxious.

Mary, on the other hand, is sitting at the feet of Jesus, listening to him. She is "being" with Jesus, enjoying intimacy with him, loving him, and taking pleasure in his presence. Her life has one center of gravity—Jesus. I suspect that if Mary were to help with the many household chores, she would not be worried or upset. Why? Her inner person has slowed down enough to focus on Jesus and to center her life on him.

Our goal is to love God with our whole being, to be consistently conscious of God through our daily life—whether we are stopped like Mary, sitting at the feet of Jesus, or active like Martha, taking care of the tasks of life.[7]

Question to Consider

What things are worrying or upsetting you today?

Prayer

Help me, O Lord, to be still and wait patiently for you (Psalm 37:7). I offer to you each of my anxieties and worries this day. Teach me to be prayerfully attentive and to rest in you as I enter into the many activities of this day. In Jesus' name, amen.

Conclude with Silence (2 minutes)

Day 4: Midday/Evening Office

Silence and Stillness before God (2 minutes)

Scripture Reading: Psalm 62:5–8

Find rest, O my soul, in God alone;

my hope comes from him.

He alone is my rock and my salvation;

he is my fortress, I will not be shaken.

My salvation and my honor depend on God;

he is my mighty rock, my refuge.

Trust in him at all times, O people;

pour out your hearts to him,

for God is our refuge. (NIV 1984)

Devotional

David, a man after God's own heart, beautifully models the seamless integration of a full emotional life with a profound contemplative life with God. He trusts in the Lord, pouring out his struggles, fears, and anguish over the lies being said about him.

In *The Cry of the Soul*, Dan Allender and Tremper Longman summarize why awareness of our feelings is so important to our relationship with God:

Ignoring our emotions is turning our back on reality; listening to our emotions ushers us into reality.

And reality is where we meet God. . . . Emotions are the language of the soul. They are the cry that gives the heart a voice. . . . However, we often turn a deaf ear—through emotional denial, distortion, or disengagement. We strain out anything disturbing in order to gain tenuous control of our inner world. We are frightened and ashamed of what leaks into our consciousness. In neglecting our intense emotions, we are false to ourselves and lose a wonderful opportunity to know God. We forget that change comes through brutal honesty and vulnerability before God.[8]

Question to Consider

What are you angry about today? Sad about? Afraid of? Pour out your response before God, trusting in him as David did.

Prayer

Lord, like David I often feel like a leaning wall, a tottering fence that is about to be knocked down! So many forces and circumstances seem to be coming against me. Help me, Lord, to find rest in you and to take shelter in you as my fortress. In Jesus' name, amen.

Conclude with Silence (2 minutes)

Day 5: Morning/Midday Office

Silence and Stillness before God (2 minutes)

Scripture Reading: John 7:2–8

But when the Jewish Festival of Tabernacles was near, Jesus' brothers said to him, "Leave Galilee and go to Judea, so that your disciples there may see the works you do. No one who wants to become a public figure acts in secret. Since you are doing these things, show yourself to the world." For even his own brothers did not believe in him.

Therefore Jesus told them, "My time is not yet here; for you any time will do. The world cannot hate you, but it hates me because I testify that its works are evil. You go to the festival. I am not yet going up to this festival, because my time has not yet fully come."

Devotional

Jesus moved slowly, not striving or rushing. He patiently waited through his adolescent and young adult years to reveal himself as the Messiah. Even then, he did not rush to be recognized. He waited patiently for his Father's timing during his short ministry. Why is it then that we hate "slow" when God appears to delight in it? Eugene Peterson offers us at least two reasons:

I am busy because I am vain. I want to appear important. Significant. What better way than to be busy? The incredible hours, the crowded schedule, and the heavy demands of my time are proof to myself—and to all who will notice—that I am important. If I go into a doctor's office and find there's no one waiting, and I see through a half-open door the doctor reading a book, I wonder if he's any good. . . .

Such experiences affect me. I live in a society in which crowded schedules and harassed conditions are evidence of importance, so I develop a crowded schedule and harassed conditions. When others notice, they acknowledge my significance, and my vanity is fed.

I am busy because I am lazy. I indolently let others decide what I will do instead of resolutely deciding myself. It was a favorite theme of C. S. Lewis that only lazy people work hard. By lazily abdicating the essential work of deciding and directing, establishing values and setting goals, other people do it for us.[9]

Question to Consider

What is one step you can take today to slow down and live more attentively to the voice of Jesus?

Prayer

Lord, grant me the grace to do one thing at a time today, without rushing or hurrying. Help me to savor the sacred in all I do, be it large or small. By the Holy Spirit within me, empower me to pause today as I move from one activity to the next. In Jesus' name, amen.

Conclude with Silence (2 minutes)

Day 5: Midday/Evening Office

Silence and Stillness before God (2 minutes)

Scripture Reading: 2 Corinthians 12:7–10

Therefore, in order to keep me from becoming conceited, I was given a thorn in my flesh, a messenger
of Satan, to torment me. Three times I pleaded with
the Lord to take it away from me. But he said to me,
"My grace is sufficient for you, for my power is made
perfect in weakness." Therefore I will boast all the more
gladly about my weaknesses, so that Christ's power may
rest on me. That is why, for Christ's sake, I delight in
weaknesses, in insults, in hardships, in persecutions,
in difficulties. For when I am weak, then I am strong.

Devotional

The Bible does not spin the flaws and weaknesses of its
heroes. Abraham lied. Hosea's wife was a prostitute.
Peter rebuked God! Noah got drunk. Jonah was a racist.
Jacob lied. John Mark deserted Paul. Elijah burned out.
Jeremiah was depressed and suicidal. Thomas doubted.
Moses had a temper. Timothy had ulcers. Even David,
one of God's beloved friends, committed adultery with
Bathsheba and murdered her husband. Yet all these people

teach us the same message: that every human being on earth, regardless of their gifts and strengths, is weak, vulnerable, and dependent on God and others.[10]

The pressure to present an image of ourselves as strong and spiritually "together" hovers over most of us. We feel guilty for not measuring up, for not making the grade. We forget that all of us are human and frail.

The apostle Paul struggled with God not answering his prayers and removing his "thorn in the flesh." Nevertheless, he thanked God for his brokenness, knowing that without it, he would have been an arrogant, "conceited" apostle. He learned, as we all must, that Christ's power is made perfect only when we are weak.

Question to Consider

How might brokenness or weakness in your life today present an opportunity for God's power to be demonstrated?

Prayer

Father, the notion of admitting to myself and to others my weaknesses and failures is very difficult. Lord, I am weak. I am dependent on you. You are God, and I am not. Help me to embrace your work in me. And may I be able to say, like Paul, "when I am weak (broken), then I am strong." In Jesus' name, amen.

Conclude with Silence (2 minutes)

Assessment

How Healthy Is Your Spirituality?

Having an emotionally unhealthy spirituality is not an all-or-nothing condition; it operates on a continuum that ranges from mild to severe, and may change from one season of life to the next. Use the list of statements that follow to get an idea of where you're at right now. Next to each statement, write down the number that best describes your response. Use the following scale:

    5 = Always true of me
    4 = Frequently true of me
    3 = Occasionally true of me
    2 = Rarely true of me
    1 = Never true of me

1. I sometimes greet people who have hurt me with a smile or a hug because I don't want to be thought of as a "bad" Christian who is unloving. _____

2. I often find myself being critical and judgmental of others, especially when they behave in ways I believe are wrong in God's eyes. _____

3. When I pray, I am more likely to ask God to bless me than I am to ask him what his will is in my life and how he wants to change me. _____

4. It can be difficult for me to identify what I am feeling inside. _____

5. When I go through a disappointment or a loss, I try to keep busy to avoid reflecting on how I feel. _____

6. I find it difficult to be honest about my fears, doubts, and hurts, so I sometimes minimize them or pretend that nothing is wrong. _____

7. I feel like I should say yes when someone asks me for help because it seems selfish or unloving to say no. _____

8. I know Jesus calls me to die to myself, but sometimes I feel tired, frustrated, and resentful about it. _____

9. I can feel guilty when I pursue things that are just for my enjoyment—art, recreation, music, beauty, etc. _____

10. To deal with conflict, I have used unhealthy patterns I learned growing up in my family, such as avoidance, putdowns, or going to a third party rather than directly to the person. _____

11. I have a hard time thanking God for painful life experiences from the past because it's difficult for me to see how he can use them for good. _____

12. I have avoided working through difficult events from my past (death of a loved one, unexpected pregnancy, divorce, addiction, financial disaster, etc.). _____

13. The busyness of life makes it difficult for me to consistently practice the spiritual disciplines of solitude and silence. _____

14. I tend to be aware of God when engaging in Christian practices at church or in quiet time but rarely when I am at work or school. _____

15. I consider some activities and areas of my life (worship, prayer, Bible reading, etc.) to be sacred, and others (doing household chores, watching television, playing sports, etc.) to be secular.   _____

16. I feel more valuable to God when I am doing something for him.   _____

17. I rarely, if ever, practice Sabbath (setting aside a twenty-four-hour period in which I stop my work and rest).   _____

18. I tend to prioritize doing things *for* God over spending time *with* God.   _____

19. I sometimes tell half-truths, or don't say anything at all, in order to avoid conflict or disapproval.   _____

20. I often say yes when I want to say no to avoid hurting someone's feelings.   _____

21. I tend to use indirect means to avoid conflict, such as sarcasm, going to a third party, or giving people the silent treatment.   _____

22. I find it difficult to talk about my weaknesses, failures, and mistakes, even with trusted friends. _____

23. I often have a hard time admitting when I'm wrong and asking for forgiveness from others. _____

24. Those close to me would say I am easily offended or hurt. _____

25. Others have commented that I tend to bite off more than I can chew. _____

26. Those close to me would say I struggle to balance family, rest, work, and play. _____

27. I find it difficult to know when to help carry someone else's burden and when to let go so they can carry their own burden. _____

28. I sometimes disapprove of how Christians from other traditions practice or talk about their faith. _____

29. It is often easier for me to see how sin has damaged others than it is for me to see how sin has damaged me. _____

30. When I see something questionable in someone's life (such as error, wrongdoing, sin),
I feel guilty if I don't correct it or offer advice
for how to fix it.   _____

Take a moment to briefly review your responses. How
many fives did you write down? Count the number of fives
on your assessment and write the total in the space pro-
vided on the right below. Note that you are counting the
number of times you wrote down five (such as three times,
five times, etc.), not adding the fives together. Then do
the same for the remaining numbers on your assessment.

Example		My Responses	
4	5 responses	_____	5 responses
11	4 responses	_____	4 responses
7	3 responses	_____	3 responses
5	2 responses	_____	2 responses
3	1 responses	_____	1 responses

What stands out most to you as you review your
responses? Although there is no definitive scoring for the
assessment, listed below are some general observations
that may help you better understand the condition of your
emotional and spiritual health right now.

If you scored mostly fours and fives, your
condition is more unhealthy than healthy, and you are

likely functioning emotionally at the level of a child or infant. You look to others to take care of you emotionally and spiritually. You likely feel uncomfortable with silence or being alone, and your prayer life is more of a duty than a delight. If all of that sounds harsh, you can at least take comfort in knowing you are far from alone. This was where I found myself after seventeen years as a Christ-follower, with a seminary degree, and eight years of pastoral experience. Growing up into spiritual and emotional adulthood takes years, even decades, not days or months. So take a deep breath. Relax. You are not alone.

If you scored mostly threes and fours, you have begun the journey, but you are likely functioning emotionally at the level of an adolescent. Your Christian life may be primarily about *doing*, not *being*, and you are feeling the effects of that. You have some awareness of how issues from your past and family of origin impact your behaviors and relationships, but more work is probably needed in this area. You tend to make quick judgments and interpretations of people's behavior. When someone hurts you, you tend to withhold forgiveness, avoid them, or cut them off. You may attend church and regularly serve others but enjoy few delights in Christ. You have done some work on developing spiritual practices to sustain you, but God may be inviting you to greater growth and a more robust inner life.

If you scored mostly ones and twos, your condition is more healthy than unhealthy, and you are likely functioning emotionally at the level of an adult. You have a healthy sense of how issues from your past and family of origin impact you, and you are able to assert your beliefs and values without being adversarial. You respect and love others without having to change them or becoming judgmental. You protect and prioritize your relationships with your spouse (if applicable), friends, and family, and relate to those around you in healthy ways. You are well on your way to integrating your *doing* for God with a solid base of *being* with him. You have moved beyond simply serving Christ to loving him and enjoying communion with him.

• • •

Wherever you find yourself, the good news is that you *can* make progress and learn to become an increasingly healthy emotionally and spiritually. In fact, God has specifically wired our bodies and neurochemistry for transformation and change—even into our nineties! So even if the truth about the current state of your emotional and spiritual health is sobering, don't be discouraged. If someone like me can learn and grow through all the failures and mistakes I've made, it is possible for anyone to make progress and develop an emotionally healthy spirituality!

Notes

The Problem of Emotionally Unhealthy Spirituality

1. Bill Bright, "The Four Spiritual Laws" (New Life Publications, 1995), 12.

2. Thomas Merton, *Thoughts in Solitude* (Boston: Shambhala, 1956), 13.

3. Quoted in Ron Sider, *The Scandal of the Evangelical Conscience: Why Are Christians Living Just Like the Rest of the World?* (Grand Rapids: Baker, 2005), 13.

4. *Scandal of the Evangelical Conscience*, 17–27.

5. *Scandal of the Evangelical Conscience*, 28–29.

6. Parker Palmer, *Let Your Life Speak: Listening for the Voice of Vocation* (San Francisco: Jossey-Bass, 2000), 30–31.

7. Quoted in Rowan Williams, *Where God Happens: Discovering Christ in One Another* (Boston: Shambhala, 2005), 14.

8. Defining and measuring emotional health or intelligence is a massive field with a wide range of opinions on what constitutes emotional maturity. Alongside my own reflections I have gleaned from such sources as Lori Gordon, *PAIRS Semester Course*, PAIRS International, curriculum guide for trainers, 437; Joseph Ciarrochi, Joseph P. Forgas, and John Mayer, eds., *Emotional*

Intelligence in Everyday Life: A Scientific Inquiry (New York: Psychology Press, 2001): and Cary Cherniss and Daniel Goleman, eds., *The Emotionally Intelligent Workplace: How to Select for, Measure, and Improve Emotional Intelligence in Individuals, Groups and Organizations* (San Francisco: Jossey-Bass, 2001). A very accessible resource is Cary Cherniss and Mitchel Adler, *Promoting Emotional Intelligence in Organizations: Make Training in Emotional Intelligence Effective* (Alexandria, VA: The American Society for Training and Development, 2000).

9. For a brief but helpful description of the contemplative stream through church history, see Richard Foster, *Streams of Living Water: Celebrating the Great Traditions of Christian Faith* (San Francisco: HarperSanFrancisco, 1998), 23–58. See also Tony Jones, *The Sacred Way: Spiritual Practices for Everyday Life* (Grand Rapids: Zondervan, 2005); Joan Chittister, *Wisdom Distilled from the Daily: Living the Rule of St. Benedict Today* (San Francisco: HarperSanFrancisco, 1990); Daniel Wolpert, *Creating a Life with God: The Call of Ancient Prayer Practices* (Nashville: Upper Room Books, 2003); and Robert E. Webber, *Ancient-Future Time: Forming Spirituality Through the Christian Year* (Grand Rapids: Baker, 2004).

Daily Offices Week One

1. Quoted in Esther De Waal, *Lost in Wonder: Rediscovering the Spiritual Art of Attentiveness* (Collegeville, MN: Liturgical Press, 2003), 19.

2. Mother Teresa, *A Simple Path* (New York: Ballantine Books, 1995), 7–8.

3. Eugene H. Peterson, *Under the Unpredictable Plant: An Exploration in Vocational Holiness* (Grand Rapids: Eerdmans, 1992), 15–16.

4. Thomas Merton, *The Wisdom of the Desert: Sayings from the Desert Fathers of the Fourth Century* (Boston: Shambhala, 1960, 2004), 1–2, 25–26.

5. R. Paul Stephens, *Down-to-Earth Spirituality: Encountering God in the Ordinary, Boring Stuff of Life* (Downers Grove, IL: InterVarsity, 2003), 12.

6. Leighton Ford, *The Attentive Life: Discovering God's Presence in All Things* (Downers Grove, IL: InterVarsity, 2008), 138–39, 173.

7. Scazzero, *Emotionally Healthy Spirituality*, 48–49.

8. Dan Allender and Tremper Longman III, *The Cry of the Soul* (Dallas: Word, 1994), 24–25.

9. Eugene Peterson, *The Contemplative Pastor: Returning to the Art of Spiritual Direction* (Grand Rapids: Eerdmans, 1989), 18–19.

10. Scazzero, *Emotionally Healthy Spirituality*, 34.

About the Author

Peter Scazzero is the founder of New Life Fellowship Church in Queens, New York City, a large, multi-racial church with more than seventy-three countries represented. After serving as senior pastor for twenty-six years, he now serves as a teaching pastor/pastor-at-large. He is the author of *The Emotionally Healthy Leader* and *The Emotionally Healthy Discipleship Course Leader's Kit,* a two-part course that is transforming churches and ministries around the world.

Pete is cofounder, along with his wife Geri, of Emotionally Healthy Spirituality, a global ministry active in over twenty-five countries. He holds a Master of Divinity from Gordon-Conwell Theological Seminary and a Doctor of Ministry in Marriage and Family.

For more information, visit emotionallyhealthy.org, or connect with Pete on Twitter @petescazzero, Facebook, or his popular podcast The Emotionally Healthy Leader.

Emotionally Healthy Spirituality

It's Impossible to Be Spiritually Mature, While Remaining Emotionally Immature

Peter Scazzero

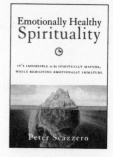

Peter Scazzero learned the hard way: you can't be spiritually mature while remaining emotionally immature. Even though he was a pastor of a growing church, he did what most people do:

- avoided conflict in the name of Christianity
- ignored his anger, sadness, and fear
- used God to run from God
- lived without boundaries

Eventually God awakened him to a biblical integration of emotional health, a relationship with Jesus, and the classic practices of contemplative spirituality. It created nothing short of a spiritual revolution, utterly transforming him and his church.

In this bestselling book Scazzero outlines his journey and the signs of emotionally unhealthy spirituality. He then goes on to provide seven biblical, reality-tested ways to break through to the revolutionary life Christ meant for you. "The combination of emotional health and contemplative spirituality," he says, "unleashes the Holy Spirit inside us so that we might experientially know the power of an authentic life in Christ."

Available in stores and online!

How Spiritually Mature Are You?

Take the
FREE Personal
Assessment
and discover what
might be holding
you back from deep
transformation.

emotionallyhealthy.org/mature